STUDY GUIDE

The Truth Mirage

STUDY GUIDE

The Truth Mirage

An Introduction to Worldview for Biblical Christians

by

FREDDY DAVIS

New International Version (NIV)
Holy Bible, New International Version®, NIV® Copyright ©1973, 1978, 1984, by Biblica, Inc.® Used by permission. All rights reserved worldwide.

The Truth Mirage
© 2019 by Freddy Davis

ISBN: 978-1-951648-00-8 (Softcover Study Guide)

Publisher:
Vision Group, Limited, The
www.LeadershipBooks.net

Published September 2019
Printed and distributed by Ingram Press

Publisher:
Vision Group, Limited, The
www.TheVisionGroupltd.com

Published September 2019
Printed and distributed by Ingram Press

All Rights Reserved. No portion of this book may be reproduced, stored in a retrieval system, or transmitted in any form or by any means-electronic, mechanical, photocopy, recording, scanning, or other—except for brief quotations in critical reviews or articles, without the prior written permission of the publisher.

Graphic Design:
KAnneDesigns

STUDY GUIDE

Table of Contents

Understanding Your Study Guide	ix
Preparations for the Study	x
The Group and Leader Preparation Tasks	xi
Guidelines for the Group	xii
Helps for Hosts	xiii
Frequently Asked Questions	xiv

Session	GROUP STUDY AND DISCUSSION	Page
I	The Importance of Understanding Worldview	1
II	What is Worldview?	7
III	The Naturalistic Worldview	13
IV	The Animistic Worldview	17
V	The Far Eastern Thought Worldview	21
VI	The Theistic Worldview and Hybrid Belief Systems	25
VII	Worldview Sources	31
VIII	Evaluating for the Truth: Lesson 1	35
IX	Evaluating for the Truth: Lesson 2	41
X	Understanding the Christian Worldview	47
XI	Using Worldview Knowledge in the World	51
XII	Putting it All Together	59
	Congratulations, Participant!	65

The Truth Mirage Study Guide

Session	LEADER'S NOTES FOR THE STUDY SESSIONS	Page
I	The Importance of Understanding Worldview	67
II	What is Worldview?	73
III	The Naturalistic Worldview	77
IV	The Animistic Worldview	81
V	The Far Eastern Thought Worldview	85
VI	The Theistic Worldview and Hybrid Belief Systems	89
VII	Worldview Sources	95
VIII	Evaluating for the Truth: Lesson 1	99
IX	Evaluating for the Truth: Lesson 2	103
X	Understanding the Christian Worldview	107
XI	Using Worldview Knowledge in the World	111
XII	Putting it All Together	117
	Congratulations, Leader!	121

Understanding Your Study Guide

This is a guide for group study of *The Truth Mirage*. With your Group's leader, we strongly encourage you to open and close both your individual preparation and group study sessions with prayer: that God will give you and each of the group's participants the wisdom necessary to use this material in ways that help each to become more knowledgeable about their own faith—and the understanding necessary to become more effective in their witness to those whom they know are not believers.

The learning features of each session include:

Review
Except for the first lesson in which you will introduce yourselves to the group, each session begins with a re-cap of the previous session's material to help maintain continuity in the study.

Consider this ...
Each part of each session has an introductory paragraph. Please read this aloud to help focus your session preparation and then, the group's discussion on the book's Chapter addressed in that part.

Video Presentation (streamed from the internet)
Each part of each session has a video-streaming lesson which presents material to the group that is specific to that part.

Discussion Questions
Each part of each session addresses the questions posed at the end of its chapter in *The Truth Mirage*. These questions are designed to encourage a vigorous group discussion to help you understand the worldview concepts, to grasp their implications and to deepen your faith life.

What Have You Learned?
Each session ends with time for you to express what you have learned from its study and share with the group how you think this can help you become more faithful in your witness in the world ... and by so doing, build each other up and embolden each other to act on what you learn.

Preparations for the Study

As you lead or participate this study of *The Truth Mirage*, do all you can to make it an informal and relaxing time.

While the material in this book is somewhat "heavy," it is designed to be very practical. With that in mind, be led, and lead yourself and your fellow participants to think deeply, while at the same time helping each other focus on the practical implications these truths hold for daily life.

Grasping the knowledge contained here will help each of you to become more knowledgeable concerning matters of faith, and cause you to become confident in your ability to stand strong in your faith—out in the world that you are *'in*, but not *of.'* (John 17:14-16)

Below are some ideas that can aid you and your leader in the session discussions. Please feel free to use these as a jumping off point to help both yourself and your fellow group participants get the most out of this study.

The Group and Leader Preparation Tasks—help from other participants is gratefully accepted!

For all participants:

1. Each week, read the corresponding chapter(s) of *The Truth Mirage* at least once all the way through and take notes on what you observe.

2. Read through the corresponding session in the Study Guide and answer each question yourself. Add to your observation notes.

3. Use your compiled observation notes as a prompt for and an aid in the class discussion. Don't be concerned about getting through the entirety of your personal observations.

For the Leader:

4. Watch the corresponding *Video Explanation* all the way through and add to your observation notes.

5. Read the Group Leader's Notes and add further to your observation notes.

During the session:

For the Leader: Your job is to be a facilitator to encourage the participants to speak what's on their hearts.

For the participants: Your job is to be a ready and willing participant. By personally being well prepared, you will be in a position to move within the discussion and take the discussion forward in case some people get stuck.

For all: Your main job is to participate and encourage discussion. This is mostly done by listening to understand, not to respond – but be ready to respond as needed.

For all participants:

6. End each group session with two questions for each group member:
    a. What did you learn new?
    b. How will this help you in your life and witness this week?

7. Open and close each session with prayer.

8. Be yourself in leading and/or participating the group session. Do it your way, as the Holy Spirit guides you, and allow others the same latitude as they seek God's leading in their lives.

9. Bathe everything and everyone in prayer. Pray during the week for every family, every group member, every session, and whatever the Holy Spirit puts on your heart to share in the group.

Guidelines for the Group

1. This is a closed-group discipleship study.

2. Attendance is by invitation only, so be courteous to your fellow members and be on time, or call if you know you are going to be late.

3. The material in this study is primarily geared for adults. If the group decides to open it up to mature youth, encourage them to take the study seriously by preparing each week ahead of time and to actively participate in the group discussions. Lead them in this by your example.

4. If there are child-care needs, the group should decide ahead of time how to handle them.

5. Everyone should feel that the group environment is a safe one. All members should agree:
   - There will be confidentiality as needed among the group members,
   - Any conflict will be resolved in a Christian manner among the group members,
   - Everyone will have their opportunity to share equally within the group, and
   - There will be no judging of one another – as is taught in Romans 14.

6. Use of electronic devices will be limited as agreed upon by the group.

Feel free to add to these as your situation warrants so that your group will be free of unnecessary distractions, and that all will feel free to contemplate and discuss the teachings of the session(s) as it relates to their own lives.

Helps for Hosts (for groups that are hosted in someone's home)

1. Don't try to do everything on your own. Delegate various responsibilities among the group members in order to develop group cohesiveness, and to avoid a situation where the host feels stressed.

2. Be prepared ahead of time with the physical niceties for each session. Have a snack, or perhaps coffee or tea, available for early comers, or for everyone as the situation allows.

3. Only invite those you feel comfortable inviting into your home.

4. In order to maintain a safe environment, the host (home owner) must always reserve the right to uninvite those they feel might jeopardize or threaten the safety or cohesion of the group.

5. Every member should be held accountable to promote a disciplined learning experience.

Frequently Asked Questions

1. Who should I invite?
    a. Participation in the group is by invitation.
    b. It is a discipleship study specifically for people who are already Christians.

2. How many weeks will the Bible study group meet?
    a. The study materials are laid to be studied over 12 sessions.
    b. The group should determine the schedule for this study in advance.

3. How long, time-wise, will each session last?
   Each group study should last for an hour to an hour and a half. Again, the group should determine this in advance.

4. What should members bring?
   Members should bring a Bible, the book, **The Truth Mirage**, and the Study Guide.

5. What about child-care?
   The group should decide in advance how it will handle this matter.

The Truth Mirage Study Guide

GROUP STUDY AND DISCUSSION TOPICS
Session-by-Session

Session 1: *The Importance of Understanding Worldview*
A Study Session in three parts on: *The Truth Mirage*, Chapters 1, 2, and 3

Open With Prayer.

Review
For this first session as a group, please spend your review-time with each person introducing themselves to the others. As a means of getting to know each other better, have each person share one thing others probably know about them, and one thing they likely don't know.

Part 1. Worldview Differences: The Basis for All Cultural Conflicts (Chapter 1)

Consider this ...
False religions are not new to our era. In Judges 2:1-23 we see the struggle Israel had with Baal worship. When they left Egypt, they *still* struggled with the worship of the gods of Egypt. And at various times they also struggled with astrology and spiritism. And in the New Testament, the Christian church struggled with the paganism of the Greek and Roman gods, the Gnostic heresy, the Judaizers, the Stoics, the Epicureans, and other false religions. Take a few moments and discuss the various instances of conflict that occurred between Israel and false religions found in the Old Testament, as well as the false gods and beliefs that the emerging new Christian church faced in New Testament times.

In modern times, the particular false religions may be different, but the struggle is exactly the same – true beliefs in conflict with false beliefs. All of the political, cultural, educational, relationship, and other conflicts we see happening in modern society are a result of the conflicting moral values that are expressions of different belief systems that are vying for prominence in society. Take a few moments and brainstorm some of the various false beliefs you have interacted with in your lives.

Video Presentation

The Truth Mirage Study Guide

Discussion Questions
Based on what is written in Chapter 1 of *The Truth Mirage*, answer and discuss the following questions.

1. What kinds of human activities are not based on a faith system?

2. What is the difference between a worldview system and a belief system?

3. What kinds of proofs are valid for legitimizing a faith system?

4. What can and cannot be proven by empiricism?

5. What kinds of conflict are based on belief systems, and what kinds are based on worldview systems?

Part 2. Why Understanding Worldview is Important (Chapter 2)

Consider this ...

If you were in Japan (or some other country whose language you did not understand), and you overheard the conversation of two individuals who were speaking that country's language, would you expect to understand what they were talking about? Of course not. You would, though, expect that the conversation was a real one and that they were speaking rational thoughts to one another. At the same time, you would not reasonably expect to understand it yourself.

A worldview is a belief language. When you are talking about your beliefs with someone else who holds your beliefs, you completely understand the meaning of the religious concepts you are dealing with (all worldview beliefs are religious beliefs). However, when you converse with someone from another worldview about your beliefs, even when speaking the same human language, communication is not taking place because the different beliefs assign different meanings to the core concepts of God, man, and salvation.

Video Presentation

Discussion Questions

Based on what is written in Chapter 2 of *The Truth Mirage*, answer and discuss the following questions.

1. What is it about a worldview that causes it to be the foundation of all our thoughts and actions?

2. How does an understanding of worldview help us more completely understand our own faith?

3. What does an understanding of worldview give us that helps us better grasp the beliefs of other faiths?

4. Why does an understanding of worldview help Christians have confidence in their own faith?

5. What is it about an understanding of worldview that makes it a practical topic of study?

Part 3. Approaches to Understanding Faith Systems (Chapter 3)

Consider this ...
Every worldview actually understands reality differently. What you understand to be real is understood as fantasy by anyone who holds a different worldview. And what anyone from another worldview considers real will appear as fantasy to you. This can be very difficult to sort out, or even understand at all, unless you have a grasp of these various worldview-faith systems and the way they approach their understanding of reality.

Video Presentation

Discussion Questions
Based on what is written in Chapter 3 of *The Truth Mirage*, answer and discuss the following questions.

1. What problems are associated with an evolutionary model of religious origins?

2. What problems are associated with an animistic model of religious origins?

3. What problems are associated with a Far Eastern Thought model of religious origins?

4. Why is a worldview approach to studying faith categories superior to any other method?

What Have You Learned?
What have you learned here that will help you be more effective in your witness to the world?

Close With Prayer: Include the needs of the group and of its members.

Session II: *What is Worldview?*

A Study Session in two parts on: *The Truth Mirage, The Truth Mirage*, Chapters 4 and 5

Open With Prayer.

Review
Please share what you learned in last week's session that you did not know before. How might you—or have you already—applied your new knowledge in your life? What impact would this have—or, already did this have—on the way you lived out your faith in your daily life?

Part 1. What is a Worldview? (Chapter 4)

Consider this ...
In Acts 17:16-21 (see the next two pages), the apostle Paul shared a message that his hearers found strange. They didn't understand "why" it was strange, only that it was. After reading this passage, discuss why a teaching, based on a different worldview, might sound strange.

Your author has had many Christians actively reject the study of worldview because they considered it to be advocating or teaching something that is not based on biblical doctrine. In rejecting a study like this, these people are showing that they don't understand the purpose of studying the topic, or even that our Acts passage is exactly such a study—done and applied by the Apostle Paul himself! In its essence, a study of worldview is not a doctrinal study, though it does help us understand doctrine. It is simply leading us to a way of categorizing faith systems in order to more easily understand and compare them. There is nothing either particularly Christian or un-Christian about understanding worldview concepts, it is just a tool to help us understand more fully. We use a worldview paradigm as a means of laying faith systems side-by-side in order to see similarities and differences, and to evaluate for truth.

Video Presentation

Discussion Questions

Based on what is written in Chapter 4 of *The Truth Mirage,* answer and discuss the following:

1. How would you define a worldview?

2. How is a worldview like an environment?

3. How is a worldview like spectacles?

4. How is a worldview like the foundation of a building?

5. How is a worldview like a language?

Acts 17:16-21 New International Version (NIV)

In Athens

> [16] While Paul was waiting for them in Athens, he was greatly distressed to see that the city was full of idols. [17] So he reasoned in the synagogue with both Jews and God-fearing Greeks, as well as in the marketplace day by day with those who happened to be there.
>
> [18] A group of Epicurean and Stoic philosophers began to debate with him. Some of them asked, "What is this babbler trying to say?" Others remarked, "He seems to be advocating foreign gods." They said this because Paul was preaching the good news about Jesus and the resurrection.
>
> [19] Then they took him and brought him to a meeting of the Areopagus, where they said to him, "May we know what this new teaching is that you are presenting? [20] You are bringing some strange ideas to our ears, and we would like to know what they mean." [21] (All the Athenians and the foreigners who lived there spent their time doing nothing but talking about and listening to the latest ideas.)

In Athens, Paul interacted with people who represented all four worldview categories:

Animists: (v. 16) The idol worship in Athens represented the Greek Animism that was prominent throughout the Roman empire.

Theists: (v. 17a) The Jews and God-fearing Greeks—who worshiped the God of the Jews – were Theists.

Naturalists: (v. 17b) The Epicureans (followers of the Greek philosopher, Epicurus) believed that there was no supernatural existence—only a material existence.

Pantheists: (v. 17b) While the Pantheism of the Stoics was somewhat different from the modern forms of Pantheism that are common in modern **Far Eastern Thought** religions, it was still a belief system that believed in an impersonal ultimate transcendent reality.

The Truth Mirage Study Guide

Part 2. What are the Worldview Possibilities? (Chapter 5)

Consider this ...
A worldview is not a belief system, it is an underlying set of beliefs that various belief systems are built upon. By being able to define the various worldview categories, we gain the ability to organize our understanding in ways that make it easy to get at the foundational beliefs of all belief systems.

Video Explanation

Discussion Questions
Based on what is written in Chapter 5 of *The Truth Mirage*, answer and discuss the following:

1. How would you define Naturalism?

2. How would you define Animism?

3. How would you define Far Eastern Thought?

4. How would you define Theism?

What Have You Learned?
What have you learned here that will help you be more effective in your witness to the world?

Close With Prayer: Include the needs of the group and of its members.

Notes:

The Truth Mirage Study Guide

Session III: *The Naturalistic Worldview*
A Study Session in one part on: *The Truth Mirage*, Chapter 6

Open With Prayer.

Review
Please share what you learned in last week's session that you did not know before. How might you—or have you already—applied your new knowledge in your life? What impact would this have—or, already did this have—on the way you lived out your faith in your daily life?

Consider this ...
Naturalism is the worldview system that is most prominent in the various institutions of modern Western societies—including America. In its essence, Naturalism is atheistic. Its beliefs directly conflict with a Theistic worldview and specifically, with Christian beliefs. They are the primary cause of the Culture War now going on in our country.

In New Testament times, Naturalism was not as prominent, but it did exist. The Epicureans that Paul debated in Athens, in Acts 17, followed a form of naturalistic belief. Read Acts 17:16-21 here and go on in that chapter to see the details of Paul's interaction with these Naturalists.

Acts 17 New International Version (NIV)

In Athens

[16] While Paul was waiting for them in Athens, he was greatly distressed to see that the city was full of idols. [17] So he reasoned in the synagogue with both Jews and God-fearing Greeks, as well as in the marketplace day by day with those who happened to be there.

[18] A group of Epicurean and Stoic philosophers began to debate with him. Some of them asked, "What is this babbler trying to say?" Others remarked, "He seems to be advocating foreign gods." They said this because Paul was preaching the good news about Jesus and the resurrection.

[19] Then they took him and brought him to a meeting of the Areopagus, where they said to him, "May we know what this new teaching is that you are presenting? [20] You are bringing some strange ideas to our ears, and we would like to know what they mean." [21] (All the Athenians and the foreigners who lived there spent their time doing nothing but talking about and listening to the latest ideas.)

[22] Paul then stood up in the meeting of the Areopagus and said: "People of Athens! I see that in every way you are very religious. [23] For as I walked around and looked carefully at your objects of worship, I even found an altar with this inscription: TO AN UNKNOWN GOD.

So, you are ignorant of the very thing you worship—and this is what I am going to proclaim to you.

24 "The God who made the world and everything in it is the Lord of heaven and earth and does not live in temples built by human hands. 25 And He is not served by human hands, as if He needed anything. Rather, He Himself gives everyone life and breath and everything else. 26 From one man He made all the nations, that they should inhabit the whole earth; and He marked out their appointed times in history and the boundaries of their lands. 27 God did this so that they would seek Him and perhaps reach out for Him and find Him, though He is not far from any one of us. 28 'For in Him we live and move and have our being.' As some of your own poets have said, 'We are His offspring.'

29 "Therefore since we are God's offspring, we should not think that the Divine Being is like gold or silver or stone—an image made by human design and skill. 30 In the past God overlooked such ignorance, but now He commands all people everywhere to repent. 31 For He has set a day when He will judge the world with justice by the man He has appointed. He has given proof of this to everyone by raising Him from the dead."

32 When they heard about the resurrection of the dead, some of them sneered, but others said, "We want to hear you again on this subject." 33 At that, Paul left the Council. 34 Some of the people became followers of Paul and believed. Among them was Dionysius, a member of the Areopagus, also a woman named Damaris, and a number of others.

Naturalistic beliefs and the worldview they produce have evolved somewhat with the advent of modern science, but it does have a very long history.

Video Presentation

Discussion Questions
Based on what is written in Chapter 6 of *The Truth Mirage*, answer and discuss the following:

1. What is the most basic premise of Naturalism?

2. How do Naturalists deal with the three essential worldview questions?

3. Why do you think Naturalists tend to be hostile to Christians?

4. Pick your favorite of the following topics and explain how Naturalism would deal with it.

Theology	Psychology	Law
Philosophy	Communication	Politics
Anthropology	Ethics and Morality	Economics
Sociology	Biology	History
	Education	

What Have You Learned?
What have you learned here that will help you be more effective in your witness to the world?

Close With Prayer: Include the needs of the group and of its members.

The Truth Mirage Study Guide

Session IV: *The Animistic Worldview*
A Study Session in one part on: *The Truth Mirage*, Chapter 7

Open With Prayer.

Review
Please share what you learned in last week's session that you did not know before. How might you—or have you already—applied your new knowledge in your life? What impact would this have—or, already did this have—on the way you lived out your faith in your daily life?

Consider this ...
Animism is not a dominant worldview in modern Western civilization, but it certainly does exist. In fact, over the last fifty years, there has been a massive increase in the number of people who follow some form of animistic belief. We have seen it increase to the extent that Wiccan headstones are now authorized for use in Arlington National Cemetery, and there is even a Pagan worship site at the U.S. Air Force Academy. So while it is not a dominant influence, it is significant in a way that has not existed before in American society.

Animistic influence does, though, have a long history. In the Old Testament we see how Israel bumped up against this worldview, as it was the basis for the worship of Baal and of the religion of ancient Egypt. In the New Testament, Greek and Roman polytheism was based on an animistic foundation. And afterwards, as the church spread into other parts of the world, Christians faced the religions based on Animism in Europe, Africa, Asia, and in North and South America.

Video Presentation

Discussion Questions
Based on what is written in Chapter 7 of *The Truth Mirage*, answer and discuss the following:

1. What is the most basic premise of Animism?

2. How do Animists deal with the three essential worldview questions?

3. What would you expect Animists to think about Christianity and why?

4. Pick one of the following topics and explain how Animism would deal with it.

Theology	Psychology	Law
Philosophy	Communication	Politics
Anthropology	Ethics and Morality	Economics
Sociology	Biology	History
	Education	

What Have You Learned?
What have you learned here that will help you be more effective in your witness to the world?

Close With Prayer: Include the needs of the group and of its members.

Notes:

The Truth Mirage Study Guide

Session V: *The Far Eastern Thought Worldview*
A Study Session in one part on: *The Truth Mirage*, Chapter 8

Open With Prayer.

Review
Please share what you learned in last week's session that you did not know before. How might you—or have you already—applied your new knowledge in your life? What impact would this have—or, already did this have—on the way you lived out your faith in your daily life?

Consider this ...
Similar to what we saw as we looked at Animism, the Far Eastern Thought worldview is also not dominant in Western society. That said, it too, has increased significantly over the last fifty years. This increase is partly due to immigration from places like India where Far Eastern Thought belief systems are dominant. It has also gained traction as religions like Buddhism have become more popular through pop culture channels such as popular movies, and the influence of various sports and other entertainment figures. Again, while it is not a dominant worldview system in the West, it has gained significant traction in America.

While Far Eastern Thought beliefs are not prominent in the Bible, the Stoicism that Paul confronted in Athens as recorded in Acts 17:16-21 was influenced by this worldview system.

Video Presentation

Discussion Questions

Based on what is written in Chapter 8 of *The Truth Mirage*, answer and discuss the following:

1. What is the most basic premise of the Far Eastern thought worldview?

2. How do FET believers understand the three essential worldview questions?

3. What would you expect FET believers to think about Christianity and why?

4. Pick your favorite of the following topics and explain how FET would deal with it.

Theology	Psychology	Law
Philosophy	Communication	Politics
Anthropology	Ethics and Morality	Economics
Sociology	Biology	History
	Education	

What Have You Learned?
What have you learned here that will help you be more effective in your witness to the world?

Close With Prayer: Include the needs of the group and of its members.

Notes

The Truth Mirage Study Guide

Session VI: *The Theistic Worldview and Hybrid Belief Systems*
A Study Session in two parts on: *The Truth Mirage*, Chapters 9 and 10

Open With Prayer.

Review
Please share what you learned in last week's session that you did not know before. How might you—or have you already—applied your new knowledge in your life? What impact would this have—or, already did this have—on the way you lived out your faith in your daily life?

Part 1. The Theistic Worldview (Chapter 9)

Consider this ...
As Paul went about his missionary work, his first stop in a new place was usually in a Jewish synagogue or worship place. He did this because people who already worshiped the God of the Old Testament were the ones who would most quickly catch on to what he was teaching—they were already Theists.

American society emerged out of a theistic worldview belief system. As such, not only do a majority of Americans claim to be Theists (though this is a decreasing majority), the very values of American society are based upon theistic notions.

That said, the Christian Theism that dominates American society is not the only form of Theism that exists here. There are cult groups like Mormonism and Jehovah's Witnesses, as well as other theistic belief systems like Judaism and Islam. As such, it is important to know not only how to recognize a theistic worldview, it is equally important to be able to distinguish between the various theistic belief systems.

Acts 17 New International Version (NIV)

In Thessalonica

[1] When Paul and his companions had passed through Amphipolis and Apollonia, they came to Thessalonica, where there was a Jewish synagogue. [2] As was his custom, Paul went into the synagogue, and on three Sabbath days he reasoned with them from the Scriptures, [3] explaining and proving that the Messiah had to suffer and rise from the dead. "This Jesus I am proclaiming to you is the Messiah," he said. [4] Some of the Jews were persuaded and joined Paul and Silas, as did a large number of God-fearing Greeks and quite a few prominent women.

⁵ But other Jews were jealous; so they rounded up some bad characters from the marketplace, formed a mob and started a riot in the city. They rushed to Jason's house in search of Paul and Silas in order to bring them out to the crowd. ⁶ But when they did not find them, they dragged Jason and some other believers before the city officials, shouting: "These men who have caused trouble all over the world have now come here, ⁷ and Jason has welcomed them into his house. They are all defying Caesar's decrees, saying that there is another king, one called Jesus." ⁸ When they heard this, the crowd and the city officials were thrown into turmoil. ⁹ Then they made Jason and the others post bond and let them go.

In Berea

¹⁰ As soon as it was night, the believers sent Paul and Silas away to Berea. On arriving there, they went to the Jewish synagogue. ¹¹ Now the Berean Jews were of more noble character than those in Thessalonica, for they received the message with great eagerness and examined the Scriptures every day to see if what Paul said was true. ¹² As a result, many of them believed, as did also a number of prominent Greek women and many Greek men.

¹³ But when the Jews in Thessalonica learned that Paul was preaching the word of God at Berea, some of them went there too, agitating the crowds and stirring them up. ¹⁴ The believers immediately sent Paul to the coast, but Silas and Timothy stayed at Berea. ¹⁵ Those who escorted Paul brought him to Athens and then left with instructions for Silas and Timothy to join him as soon as possible.

Video Presentation

Discussion Questions

Based on what is written in Chapter 9 of *The Truth Mirage*, answer and discuss the following:

1. What is the most basic premise of a theistic worldview?

2. How do Theists answer the three essential worldview questions?

3. What would you expect various Theists to believe about Christianity and why?

4. Pick your favorite of the following topics and explain it using a theistic understanding of reality.

Theology	Psychology	Law
Philosophy	Communication	Politics
Anthropology	Ethics and Morality	Economics
Sociology	Biology	History
	Education	

Part 2. Hybrid Worldview Beliefs (Chapter 10)

Consider this ...
As was noted earlier, every worldview literally contradicts every other worldview. Worldview beliefs are completely exclusive. For example: It is impossible for God to exist and not exist at the same time. It is impossible for human beings to be impersonal life forms and personal beings at the same time. It is impossible for the ultimate in life to consist exclusively of God's will and of individual human desires at the same time.

Hybrid belief systems are attempts to combine beliefs from two or more worldview systems. That being the case, every single one is founded upon irreconcilable contradictory beliefs. This can prove difficult to sort out without a specific understanding of worldview concepts. It seems we human beings have an uncanny ability to ignore the cognitive dissonance inherent in accepting hybridized beliefs.

We don't see any formal hybrid belief systems found in the Bible, but we do see a considerable amount of hybridization of beliefs as we study. For instance, Israel claimed belief in the God of the Bible, yet they often slipped back into pagan worship and attempted to hold the two contradictory beliefs together at the same time.

Video Presentation

Discussion Questions
Based on what is written in Chapter 10 of *The Truth Mirage*, answer and discuss the following:

1. What is the greatest problem hybrid belief systems face?

2. How do people manage to overcome the biggest problem facing hybrid belief systems?

3. What worldview category do hybrid belief systems fall into?

4. Of the hybrid systems listed above, which do you think is the most prominent? Which is the most accepted?

What Have You Learned?
What have you learned here that will help you be more effective in your witness to the world?

Close With Prayer: Include the needs of the group and of its members.

The Truth Mirage Study Guide

Session VII: *Worldview Sources*
A Study Session in two parts on: *The Truth Mirage*, Chapters 11 and 12

Open With Prayer.

Review
Please share what you learned in last week's session that you did not know before. How might you—or have you already—applied your new knowledge in your life? What impact would this have—or, already did this have—on the way you lived out your faith in your daily life?

Part 1. How do People Arrive at a Worldview? (Chapter 11)

Consider this ...
Even though worldview beliefs are the most deeply held beliefs an individual has, for the most part, people are completely unaware of their own worldview beliefs. The reason for this is that worldview beliefs define reality for an individual. It is hard to even imagine that something is real when you know in your heart of hearts that it is a fantasy. Because of that, individuals rarely even think about their worldview beliefs, much less challenge their viability.

There actually are instances in the Bible where people stand up against the truth and even persecute those who follow God because of their own strong commitment to their own beliefs.

We are confronted with these nagging questions:
- How does it happen that every individual has a set of worldview beliefs.
- Where do those beliefs come from?
- With so many different beliefs in existence, how is it possible that every person is so convinced that his or her own is the truth?

Video Presentation

The Truth Mirage Study Guide

Discussion Questions
Based on what is written in Chapter 11 of *The Truth Mirage*, answer and discuss the following:

1. What is the default worldview of every person on earth?

2. Why would a clash of worldviews cause some people to convert to a different belief?

3. What is necessary if a person is going to make a deliberate choice about what worldview belief to follow?

Part 2. Worldview Authority Sources (Chapter 12)

Consider this ...
Every belief system in existence is built upon the foundation of some authority source. There is a generic authority source for every worldview system, and a very specific authority source for most belief systems. It is actually possible learn about and evaluate these authority sources as a way to examine the truth or falsity of any given faith system.

There actually are numerous non-biblical belief systems mentioned in the Bible. Some of these include Baal worship, worship of the Egyptian gods, Gnosticism, Epicureanism, worship of Greek gods, and the like.

Can you think of any of the non-biblical, belief systems of today? ... and their authority sources? ... their worldview category?

Video Presentation

Discussion Questions
Based on what is written in Chapter 12 of *The Truth Mirage,* answer and discuss the following:

1. What are the four possible worldview authority sources and what distinguishes each one?

2. Why is it important to distinguish between big-picture and small-picture authority sources?

What Have You Learned?
What have you learned here that will help you be more effective in your witness to the world?

Close With Prayer: Include the needs of the group and of its members.

The Truth Mirage Study Guide

Session VIII: *Evaluating for Truth—Lesson 1*
A Study Session in three parts on: *The Truth Mirage*, Chapters 13, 14, and 15

Open With Prayer.

Review
Please share what you learned in last week's session that you did not know before. How might you—or have you already—applied your new knowledge in your life? What impact would this have—or, already did this have—on the way you lived out your faith in your daily life?

Part 1. Evaluating for the Truth of a Worldview (Chapter 13)

Consider this ...
There is a way reality is actually structured, and we cannot help but live life based on that actual structure. While it is possible for people to hold beliefs that contradict that reality, it is impossible to actually live as if reality is different from what it is. By comparing belief systems or worldview beliefs to the actual way we live, because of the constraints of the material reality we live within, we can see where various worldview or belief systems deviate from actual reality.

Video Presentation

Discussion Questions
Based on what is written in Chapter 13 of *The Truth Mirage*, answer and discuss the following:

1. Why is it important for human experience and an individual's beliefs to match up?

2. What happens when human experience and individual beliefs don't match up?

Part 2. Evaluating the Truth of Naturalism (Chapter 14)

Consider this ...

Naturalistic beliefs correspond to the way humans experience reality in some ways, but there are other places where it does not. These non-corresponding places are a strong indication that a naturalistic worldview does not reflect the way reality is actually organized. You, no doubt, know people who are Naturalists and make no bones about being Atheists, Secular Humanists, or the like. Should you confront people who hold these beliefs, and if so, what should be your point of contact with them?

Table 14.1. Evaluation: The Truth of Naturalism.

Human Experience	Naturalist's Experience	Do They Match?
Personal, self-aware beings	Yes	No
Sense of transcendence	Yes	No
Life in relationships	Yes	No
Spiritual Qualities	Yes	No
Life Based on Natural Laws	Yes	Yes
Capable of Knowledge	Yes	No
Sense of Morality	Yes	No
Experience Time as Linear	Yes	Yes
Experience the World as Objective	Yes	Yes

Video Presentation

Discussion Questions

Based on what is written in Chapter 14 of *The Truth Mirage,* answer and discuss the following:

1. In what ways does naturalistic belief match up with human experience?

2. In what ways does naturalistic belief not match up with human experience?

3. What does the fact that there are places where naturalistic belief does and does not match up with human experience tell you about the viability of Naturalism?

The Truth Mirage Study Guide

Part 3. Evaluating the Truth of Animism (Chapter 15)

Consider this ...

Animism also recognizes certain elements of reality, but because of its worldview beliefs, it is often not able to make a clear distinction between the action of natural laws and what they think are the actions of the spirits. The inability to make that distinction is a strong indication that Animism does not represent the actual structure of reality. Who do you know who follows some form of Animistic belief? Should you confront people who hold these beliefs, and if so, what should be your point of contact with them?

Table 15-1. Evaluation: The Truth of Animism

Human Experience	Animist's Experience	Do They Match?
Personal, self-aware beings	Yes	Yes
Sense of transcendence	Yes	Yes
Life in relationships	Yes	Yes
Spiritual Qualities	Yes	Partially
Life Based on Natural Laws	Yes	Partially
Capable of Knowledge	Yes	Partially
Sense of Morality	Yes	Yes
Experience Time as Linear	Yes	Yes
Experience the World as Objective	Yes	Partially

Video Presentation

Session VIII

Discussion Questions
Based on what is written in Chapter 15 of *The Truth Mirage,* answer and discuss the following:

1. In what ways does animistic belief match up with human experience?

2. In what ways does animistic belief not match up with human experience?

3. What does the fact that there are places where animistic belief does and does not match up with human experience tell you about the viability of Animism?

What Have You Learned?
What have you learned here that will help you be more effective in your witness to the world?

Close With Prayer: Include the needs of the group and of its members.

The Truth Mirage Study Guide

Session 18: *Evaluating for Truth – Lesson 2*
A Study Session in two parts on: *The Truth Mirage*, Chapters 16 and 17

Open With Prayer.

Review
Please share what you learned in last week's session that you did not know before. How might you—or have you already—applied your new knowledge in your life? What impact would this have—or, already did this have—on the way you lived out your faith in your daily life?

Part 1. Evaluating the Truth of Far Eastern Thought (Chapter 16)

Consider this ...
Because Far Eastern Thought considers the material universe to be illusory, there is NO PLACE where human experience and Far Eastern Thought beliefs align.

This is a very powerful sign that Far Eastern Thought does not reflect reality's actual structure. Who do you know who follows some form of Far Eastern Thought belief? Should you confront people who hold these beliefs, and if so, what should be your point of contact with them?

Table 16-1. Evaluation: The Truth of Far Eastern Thought (FET)

Human Experience	FET Experience	Do They Match?
Personal, self-aware beings	Yes	No
Sense of transcendence	Yes	No
Life in relationships	Yes	No
Spiritual Qualities	Yes	No
Life Based on Natural Laws	Yes	No
Capable of Knowledge	Yes	No
Sense of Morality	Yes	No
Experience Time as Linear	Yes	No
Experience the World as Objective	Yes	No

Video Presentation

The Truth Mirage Study Guide

Discussion Questions
Based on what is written in Chapter 16 of *The Truth Mirage*, answer and discuss the following:

1. In what ways does Far Eastern Thought belief match up with human experience?

2. In what ways does Far Eastern Thought belief not match up with human experience?

3. What does the fact that there are no places where Far Eastern Thought belief matches up with human experience tell you about the viability of Far Eastern Thought?

Part 2. Evaluating the Truth of Theism (Chapter 17)

Consider this ...

Human experience and the beliefs of Theism match up at every point. This is a powerful indication that reality is structured according to a theistic worldview. We must be careful to note, however, that this does not mean that every theistic belief system represents the truth. That must be tested in a different way. However, the truth about how reality is structured is based upon a theistic worldview.

Table 17-1. Evaluation: The Truth of Theism

Human Experience	Theist's Experience	Do They Match?
Personal, self-aware beings	Yes	Yes
Sense of transcendence	Yes	Yes
Life in relationships	Yes	Yes
Spiritual Qualities	Yes	Yes
Life Based on Natural Laws	Yes	Yes
Capable of Knowledge	Yes	Yes
Sense of Morality	Yes	Yes
Experience Time as Linear	Yes	Yes
Experience the World as Objective	Yes	Yes

Video Presentation

Discussion Questions

Based on what is written in Chapter 17 of *The Truth Mirage*, answer and discuss the following:

1. In what ways does theistic belief match up with human experience?

2. In what ways does theistic belief not match up with human experience?

3. What does the fact that theistic beliefs match up with human experience at every point tell you about the viability of Theism?

What Have You Learned?

What have you learned here that will help you be more effective in your witness to the world?

Close With Prayer: Include the needs of the group and of its members.

Notes

The Truth Mirage Study Guide

Session 8: *Understanding the Christian Worldview*
A Study Session in two parts on: *The Truth Mirage*, Chapters 18 and 19

Open With Prayer.

Review
Please share what you learned in last week's session that you did not know before. How might you—or have you already—applied your new knowledge in your life? What impact would this have—or, already did this have—on the way you lived out your faith in your daily life?

Part 1. The Structure of Truth – Biblical Christianity (Chapter 18)

Consider this ...
There is a way that reality is actually structured and that way is represented by the teachings of biblical Christianity. We can learn the worldview beliefs of Christianity by looking at how the Bible answers the three worldview questions. An important element of that relates to our ability to see it in its historical context by tracing the biblical story of creation, the Fall, life after the Fall, redemption, and eternity.

Video Presentation

Discussion Questions
Based on what is written in Chapter 18 of *The Truth Mirage*, answer and discuss the following:

1. What does the Bible teach about God?

2. What does the Bible teach about humanity?

3. What does the Bible teach about salvation?

4. Based on a narrative description, what is the big-picture context of reality?

The Truth Mirage Study Guide

Part 2. Why Christians Believe Different Things (Chapter 19)

Consider this ...

As we look at the Christian faith, it becomes obvious very quickly that there are a lot of conflicting beliefs within the faith. In fact, these differences are often the reason different denominations exist. A lot of the differences we see are mere matters of personal preference. However, others are the result of differing interpretations of Scripture as it relates to various Christian doctrines.

Sadly, many Christians struggle mightily with not only the fact that differences exist, but also with the magnitude of those differences. While these different matters are important to varying degrees, no difference that exists outside of the genuine core of essential Christian beliefs should cause division within the body of Christ.

Video Presentation

Discussion Questions

Based on what is written in Chapter 19 of **The Truth Mirage**, answer and discuss the following:

1. What are the essentials of the Christian faith?

2. What kinds of non-essentials still tend to divide Christians and how can this be avoided?

3. What evidence exists that some who call themselves Christians are not?

What Have You Learned?
What have you learned here that will help you be more effective in your witness to the world?

Close With Prayer: Include the needs of the group and of its members.

The Truth Mirage Study Guide

Session 8I: *Using Worldview Knowledge in the World*
A Study Session in three parts on: *The Truth Mirage*, Chapters 20, 21, and 22

Open With Prayer.

Review
Please share what you learned in last week's session that you did not know before. How might you—or have you already—applied your new knowledge in your life? What impact would this have—or, already did this have—on the way you lived out your faith in your daily life?

Part 1. What Does Worldview Conflict Look Like? (Chapter 20)

Consider this ...
There are a lot of conflicts in the world, and many of them are of little consequence.

But conflicts that are based on worldview differences are religious battles regarding beliefs that people are often willing to even go to war over.

Christians need to not only be able to recognize these differences, but also need to be able to engage them in a way that is consistent with biblical beliefs.

Video Presentation

Discussion Questions
Based on what is written in Chapter 20 of *The Truth Mirage*, answer and discuss the following:

1. What is the difference between culture wars and worldview wars?

2. To really understand the issues that are fought over in the culture wars, what is necessary?

3. How can culture wars actually be won?

Part 2. How Can Christians Be Sure They Hold a Biblical Worldview? (Chapter 21)

Consider this ...
A biblical worldview is not about which church an individual Christians attends. It is about how one answers the three essential worldview questions. Those who answer those questions based on biblical teachings are the ones who hold a biblical worldview.

The Three Worldview Questions:
1. What Is the Nature of Ultimate Reality?

2. What is a Human Being?

3. What Is the Ultimate a Human Being Can Get Out of this Life?

Video Presentation

Discussion Questions

Based on what is written in Chapter 21 of *The Truth Mirage*, answer and discuss the following:

1. How does the Bible answer the three essential worldview questions?

2. What does a person's lifestyle tell you about their worldview beliefs?

3. How does God work in individual believer's lives to equip them to carry out his will in daily life?

Part 3. How Can Christians Effectively Fight the Worldview War? (Chapter 22)

Consider this ...
Worldview conflicts are battles over the heart, mind, and soul of human beings. God has called Christians to be engaged in those battles in order to wipe away the mirages of false beliefs in order to help people enter into a personal relationship with God through Jesus Christ. To do this, we need to be intentional by learning the knowledge and skills necessary to engage the battle, and to develop a plan to fight it.

Video Presentation

Discussion Questions
Based on what is written in Chapter 22 of *The Truth Mirage,* answer and discuss the following:

1. What is the essential knowledge base Christians must possess to fulfill God's purpose in life?

2. What kinds of skills are necessary for Christians to develop in order to fulfill God's purpose in life?

3. How does one go about developing an individual plan for accomplishing the will of God in life?

4. What must a person ultimately be willing to do in order to accomplish God's purpose?

Preparation for Next Week
Please search the news sites and bring two articles that have to do with worldview issues. These articles can be about how various moral issues are expressed in society, explanations of various religions, cults, or philosophies that are being promoted in society, or beliefs being promoted in politics, the media, education, business, entertainment, family, or religion. The group will be discussing these articles during the session next week.

What Have You Learned?
What have you learned here that will help you be more effective in your witness to the world?

Close With Prayer: Include the needs of the group and of its members.

Notes

Session XII: *Putting it All Together*
A Study Session in one part on: *The Truth Mirage*

Open With Prayer.

Review

Please share what you learned in last week's session that you did not know before. How might you—or have you already—applied your new knowledge in your life? What impact would this have—or, already did this have—on the way you lived out your faith in your daily life?

This is the last session of this study, and its purpose is to help you see the big picture of the worldview process.

Consider ...

The concept of worldview can be broken down into many parts to help you understand it more completely, but ultimately it needs to be consolidated into a broad paradigm in order to use those parts to understand the various faith systems. Particularly think about:

- The importance of understanding worldview
- The definition of worldview
- The four categories (plus hybrids) of worldview faith systems
- The sources of worldview beliefs
- How to evaluate for the truth of the various worldview systems
- How the Christian faith fits into the worldview paradigm, and
- The practical implications and applications of a worldview paradigm

Acts 17 New International Version (NIV)

In Thessalonica

17 When Paul and his companions had passed through Amphipolis and Apollonia, they came to Thessalonica, where there was a Jewish synagogue. ² As was his custom, Paul went into the synagogue, and on three Sabbath days he reasoned with them from the Scriptures, ³ explaining and proving that the Messiah had to suffer and rise from the dead. "This Jesus I am proclaiming to you is the Messiah," he said. ⁴ Some of the Jews were persuaded and joined Paul and Silas, as did a large number of God-fearing Greeks and quite a few prominent women.

⁵ But other Jews were jealous; so they rounded up some bad characters from the marketplace, formed a mob and started a riot in the city. They rushed to Jason's house in search of Paul and Silas in order to bring them out to the crowd.[a] ⁶ But when they did not find them, they dragged Jason and some other believers before the city officials, shouting: "These men who

have caused trouble all over the world have now come here, ⁷ and Jason has welcomed them into his house. They are all defying Caesar's decrees, saying that there is another king, one called Jesus." ⁸ When they heard this, the crowd and the city officials were thrown into turmoil. ⁹ Then they made Jason and the others post bond and let them go.

In Berea

¹⁰ As soon as it was night, the believers sent Paul and Silas away to Berea. On arriving there, they went to the Jewish synagogue. ¹¹ Now the Berean Jews were of more noble character than those in Thessalonica, for they received the message with great eagerness and examined the Scriptures every day to see if what Paul said was true. ¹² As a result, many of them believed, as did also a number of prominent Greek women and many Greek men.

¹³ But when the Jews in Thessalonica learned that Paul was preaching the word of God at Berea, some of them went there too, agitating the crowds and stirring them up. ¹⁴ The believers immediately sent Paul to the coast, but Silas and Timothy stayed at Berea. ¹⁵ Those who escorted Paul brought him to Athens and then left with instructions for Silas and Timothy to join him as soon as possible.

In Athens

¹⁶ While Paul was waiting for them in Athens, he was greatly distressed to see that the city was full of idols. ¹⁷ So he reasoned in the synagogue with both Jews and God-fearing Greeks, as well as in the marketplace day by day with those who happened to be there.

¹⁸ A group of Epicurean and Stoic philosophers began to debate with him. Some of them asked, "What is this babbler trying to say?" Others remarked, "He seems to be advocating foreign gods." They said this because Paul was preaching the good news about Jesus and the resurrection.

¹⁹ Then they took him and brought him to a meeting of the Areopagus, where they said to him, "May we know what this new teaching is that you are presenting? ²⁰ You are bringing some strange ideas to our ears, and we would like to know what they mean." ²¹ (All the Athenians and the foreigners who lived there spent their time doing nothing but talking about and listening to the latest ideas.)

²² Paul then stood up in the meeting of the Areopagus and said: "People of Athens! I see that in every way you are very religious. ²³ For as I walked around and looked carefully at your objects of worship, I even found an altar with this inscription: TO AN UNKNOWN GOD.

SO, YOU ARE IGNORANT OF THE VERY THING YOU WORSHIP—AND THIS IS WHAT I AM GOING TO PROCLAIM TO YOU.

²⁴ "The God who made the world and everything in it is the Lord of heaven and earth and does not live in temples built by human hands. ²⁵ And He is not served by human hands, as if He needed anything. Rather, He Himself gives everyone life and breath and everything else.

²⁶ From one man He made all the nations, that they should inhabit the whole earth; and He marked out their appointed times in history and the boundaries of their lands. ²⁷ God did this so that they would seek Him and perhaps reach out for Him and find Him, though He is not far from any one of us. ²⁸ 'For in Him we live and move and have our being.' As some of your own poets have said, 'We are His offspring.'

²⁹ "Therefore since we are God's offspring, we should not think that the Divine Being is like gold or silver or stone—an image made by human design and skill. ³⁰ In the past God overlooked such ignorance, but now He commands all people everywhere to repent. ³¹ For He has set a day when He will judge the world with justice by the man He has appointed. He has given proof of this to everyone by raising Him from the dead."

³² When they heard about the resurrection of the dead, some of them sneered, but others said, "We want to hear you again on this subject." ³³ At that, Paul left the Council. ³⁴ Some of the people became followers of Paul and believed. Among them was Dionysius, a member of the Areopagus, also a woman named Damaris, and a number of others.

Video Presentation

Worldview Conflict in Modern Society

There are headlines every day that illustrate the beliefs of various worldview systems, and the conflict between these various systems. Go to newspapers, news websites, and other resources and find articles that illustrate these conflicts.

Discuss the worldview beliefs that are mentioned and the implications of those beliefs as they play out in life. The articles can be about:

- the expression of various moral issues in society;
- various religions, cults, or philosophies that are being promoted in society; or
- beliefs being promoted in politics, the media, education, business, entertainment, family, and religion.

Use all the knowledge you have gained to analyze and discuss the articles, along with what Christians can do to promote Christ in the culture.

What Have You Learned?
What have you learned here that will help you be more effective in your witness to the world?

Close With Prayer: Include the needs of the group and of its members.

Notes

The Truth Mirage Study Guide

Congratulations!

For completing your study of

The Truth Mirage.

Without your hard work through this study, all of our hard work in producing it goes for naught.

We try to make your personal preparations and group study experience as profitable for you as we can—but we know that your experience with it, with your group, and its materials can add even more benefit to others who will follow you in this and other studies we produce.

Would you share with us what we could do to improve our courseware?

Please share your suggestions with the Authors and Editors at **GetPublished.pro** that we may fold them into this and following works to make your and your fellow participants and leaders experience with our materials more fulfilling.

Just visit our contact page, GetPublished.pro (click on: CONTACT US) and share with us right on this page, send us a letter—or email us with your suggestions!

All comments are welcome and will help us produce better books, study guides, and video supplements.

Thank you for your feedback comments—and for working your way through *The Truth Mirage* and its study. Our prayers are with you that you may use its content in your own life to understand the many ways the world understands reality and how this affects our ability to understand each other—as those worldviews that used to be way out in the foreign mission field are now all right here among us!

LEADER'S TEACHING NOTES
SESSION BY SESSION

Session 1: *The Importance of Understanding Worldview*
A Study Session in three parts on: *The Truth Mirage*, Chapters 1, 2, and 3

WARNING: Three chapters and three parts to this session—move among them efficiently.

Open the Session with prayer ... that God will give each of us:
- the wisdom necessary to use today's material in ways that help each of us become more knowledgeable about our own faith,
  —and—
- the understanding necessary to become more effective in their witness to those whom they know are not believers.

Review
For this first session as a group, have each person introduce themselves to one to another, sharing one thing others probably know about them, and one thing they likely don't know.

Part 1. Worldview Differences: The Basis for All Cultural Conflicts (Chapter 1)

Opening the Conversation: ...
With the opening considerations of this first Part/Chapter in the Participant's Guide portion, have group members take a few moments to brainstorm some of the various false beliefs you/they have interacted with in your/their lives.

Discussion Questions
1. *What kinds of human activities are not based on a faith system?*
   ALL human activity, once engaged, is based on a faith system. Everyone acts, in every part of life, based on what they consider to be the real and true way reality is organized.

2. *What is the difference between a worldview system and a belief system?*
   A worldview system defines how people understand what is real and what is fantasy.
   A belief system defines the parameters of specific religions, cults, and philosophies.

3. *What kinds of proofs are valid for legitimizing a faith system?*
   Empirical knowledge, logic, deduction, and human experience comprise the types of evidence that supports the validity of a faith system, and all must work together.

4. *What can and cannot be proven by empiricism?*
   Empirical science is able to help us understand the operation of the material universe. Empiricism is unable to prove anything that operates outside the realm of the laws of the natural universe.

5. *What kinds of conflict are based on belief systems, and what kinds are based on worldview systems?*
   Typically, shallow, relatively unimportant conflicts are based on belief system beliefs. As people's identity is tied to their worldview beliefs; however, battles at this level tend to be much more intense.

Part 2. Why Understanding Worldview is Important (Chapter 2)

Moving the Conversation to the next part: ...
With our opening considerations of this Part/Chapter, if you really wanted to understand the conversation of people who spoke another language, what would you have to do? (Learn the language, understand their use of words you have in common, learn their assumed concepts, ...)

Discussion Questions

1. *What is it about a worldview that causes it to be the foundation of all our thoughts and actions?*
   Worldview beliefs are the very foundation of an individual's understanding of self. They are the most foundational beliefs people hold. They determine what individuals understand to be reality and fantasy.

2. *How does an understanding of worldview help us more completely understand our own faith?*
   An understanding of worldview informs us as to the essential core beliefs of our faith.

3. *What does an understanding of worldview give us that helps us better grasp the beliefs of other faiths?*
   An understanding of worldview helps us understand the essential core beliefs of other faiths in a way that helps us bridge the gap between our faith and another.

4. *Why does an understanding of worldview help Christians have confidence in their faith?*
   An understanding of worldview helps us understand why the Christian faith is the truth and other faiths are not.

5. *What is it about an understanding of worldview that makes it a practical topic of study?*
   An understanding of worldview provides confidence concerning the truthfulness of our Christian faith, and gives us tools to bridge the conceptual gap between our faith and others.

Part 3. Approaches to Understanding Faith Systems (Chapter 3)

Moving the Conversation to the next part: ...
With our opening considerations for this Part/Chapter: Have you ever heard someone make the statement that "Christian beliefs are narrow-minded?" How is a Christian supposed to deal with that objection? (Help the individual to recognize that EVERY belief is narrow-minded.)

Discussion Questions

    1. What problems are associated with an evolutionary model of religious origins?
        The main problem with the evolutionary model is that there is no way to be sure this approach is correct. It assumes an evolutionary sequence, but one cannot know for sure.

    2. What problems are associated with an animistic model of religious origins?
        Generally, it would never occur to Animists to even consider the idea of religious origins.

    3. What problems are associated with a Far Eastern Thought model of religious origins?
        The greatest problem with a Far Eastern Thought model of origins is that the faith system does not allow for conscious thought in an ultimate sense. Ultimate reality is believed to be impersonal and immaterial, and the entirety of the natural universe is illusory.

    4. Why is a worldview approach to studying faith categories superior to any other method?
        The worldview paradigm provides a means for evaluating for truth, and for comparing various faith systems to one another.

What Have You Learned?
What have you learned here that will help you be more effective in your witness to the world?

Close the Session with prayer ... that God will give each of us
- the wisdom necessary to use today's material in ways that help each of us become more knowledgeable about our own faith,
- the understanding necessary to become more effective in their witness to those whom they know are not believers,
  —and—
- ... other prayer needs of the group or its members.

Notes

The Truth Mirage Leadership Notes

Session II: *What is Worldview?*
A Study Session in two parts on: *The Truth Mirage, The Truth Mirage,* Chapters 4 and 5

WARNING: Two chapters and two parts to this session – again, move among them efficiently.

Open the Session with prayer … that God will give each of us
- the wisdom necessary to use today's material in ways that help each of us become more knowledgeable about our own faith,
  —and—
- the understanding necessary to become more effective in their witness to those whom they know are not believers.

Review … ask the participants:
- What did you learn in last week's session that you did not know before?
- How might you—or have you already—applied your new knowledge in your life?
- What impact would this have—or, already did this have—on the way you lived out your faith in your daily life?

Part 1. What is a Worldview? (Chapter 4)

Opening the Conversation: …
With our opening considerations of this Part/Chapter, what worldviews were present on in Athens among the people with whom Paul interacted? [This would have included Greek Polytheists (Animists), Jews (Theists), Epicureans (Naturalists), and Stoics (Pantheists).]

Discussion Questions

1. *How would you define a worldview?*
   A worldview is the assumptions people make about the nature of reality. Assumptions are matters that seem so obvious that they are not even questioned. The nature of reality refers to those things that are real – as opposed to things that are fantasy.

2. *How is a worldview like an environment?*
   A worldview is a belief environment. It totally defines one's beliefs to the extent that it is impossible for anything to exist outside of that environment.

3. How is a worldview like spectacles?
   A worldview is like a belief lens. When one evaluates every part of life, it is evaluated on the basis of one's worldview beliefs. As such, it filters out notions that do not fit with the worldview beliefs.

4. How is a worldview like the foundation of a building?
   A worldview is like a belief foundation. A person's worldview beliefs define the boundaries of what is real vs. what is fantasy. When one interacts with beliefs that do not fit with the foundation, the foundation will not support them.

5. How is a worldview like a language?
   A worldview is like a belief language. Concepts that do not correspond with a person's worldview beliefs seem incomprehensible.

Session II

Part 2. What are the Worldview Possibilities? (Chapter 5)

Opening the Conversation: ...
With our opening considerations of this Part/Chapter have the class members memorize the four worldview categories and their definitions.

Discussion Questions

1. *How would you define Naturalism?*
   Naturalism is the belief that the natural universe is all that exists.

2. *How would you define Animism?*
   Animism is the belief that there exists both a material and a spirit world that symbiotically interact with one another. What happens in one part affects what happens in the other part.

3. *How would you define Far Eastern Thought?*
   Far Eastern Thought is the belief that Ultimate reality is a transcendent impersonal life force, and that the natural universe is an illusory expression of reality. With that, the natural universe actually does exist, but does not exist in a form that corresponds with actual reality. Actual reality is immaterial and impersonal.

4. *How would you define Theism?*
   Theism is the belief that an actual transcendent God exists who is the creator and sustainer of the natural universe.

What Have You Learned?
What have you learned here that will help you be more effective in your witness to the world?

Close the Session with prayer ... that God will give each of us
- the wisdom necessary to use today's material in ways that help each of us become more knowledgeable about our own faith,
- the understanding necessary to become more effective in their witness to those whom they know are not believers,
  —and—
- ... other prayer needs of the group or its members.

The Truth Mirage Leadership Notes

SESSION III: *The Naturalistic Worldview*
A Study Session in one part on: *The Truth Mirage*, Chapter 6

Open the Session with prayer ... that God will give each of us
- the wisdom necessary to use today's material in ways that help each of us become more knowledgeable about our own faith,
  —and—
- the understanding necessary to become more effective in their witness to those whom they know are not believers.

Review ... ask the participants:
- What did you learn in last week's session that you did not know before?
- How might you—or have you already—applied your new knowledge in your life?
- What impact would this have—or, already did this have—on the way you lived out your faith in your daily life?

The Naturalistic Worldview (Chapter 6)

Opening the Conversation: ...
With our opening considerations of this Part/Chapter, how did the Apostle Paul (in Acts 17, see the passage as presented in the Session 2 and 3 material) frame his interactions for the naturalistic Epicurean philosophers in the Athens Areopagus so they might understand his preaching? (While the Epicureans were not Animists, they were very familiar with animistic concepts as it was the dominant worldview in that part of the world at that time. Thus, Paul's use of an animistic concept would have been grasped by the Epicureans.)

Discussion Questions

1. *What is the most basic premise of Naturalism?*
   The most basic premise of Naturalism is that the natural universe is all that exists.

2. *How do Naturalists deal with the three essential worldview questions?*
   a. There is no such thing as a transcendent reality – including God.
   b. Human beings are purely natural animals with a highly evolved brain.
   c. The ultimate one can achieve in life on a macro level is survival. On a personal level, the ultimate is personal meaning and fulfillment. This is achieved by doing whatever it takes to accomplish it.

3. Why do you think Naturalists tend to be hostile to Christians?
> As a religious faith, Naturalism has a natural antagonism to other religious faiths. It is especially hostile to Christianity because the moral expectations of the Christian faith are diametrically opposed to naturalistic morality.

4. Pick one of the following topics and explain how Naturalism would deal with it.

Theology: God does not exist.

Philosophy:
a. Reality is based completely on natural laws, and human reason is the only way it is possible to get at truth.
b. The ability to gain and use knowledge rests completely on the evolutionary development of the brain.
c. Values are purely the creation of humanity based on felt needs in any given situation. They are strictly functional and can be changed as the situation dictates.

Anthropology: Human social organization is purely an evolutionary expression of humanity's quest for survival.

Sociology: There is no objective purpose for man's existence. He is purely an evolved creature that developed in a way that caused human beings to be social creatures for the purpose of survival.

Psychology: The human soul is purely a physical expression of the human person. The solution for psychological problems is found purely in fixing wrong thinking by using behavioral techniques.

Communication: The human capacity for self-consciousness is strictly the result of naturalistic evolution. Thus, the human brain has evolved to the place where self-conscious processing of information has become possible.

Ethics and Morality: Ethics and morality are purely human constructs based on the evolutionary development of human beings as they seek to promote survival. There is no such thing as objective right and wrong, as there is no objective law giver. All morality is relative to the situation.

Biology:
a. All life came into existence by natural means.
b. All life forms developed based on naturalistic evolution.
c. The survival of the species (the 'collective') is more important than the survival (or other needs) of the individual.

Law: Since there is no objective basis for any kind of morality, the purpose of laws is merely to maintain order in society so as to promote its survival. Typically, those who hold power are the ones who determine what laws are created and maintained.

Politics: The interests of the collective take priority over the interests of the individual. Those who hold political power are the ones who hold sway over society. Society's citizens should defer to those in power.

Economics: A collectivist philosophy dominates the naturalistic approach to economics. Society's resources should be distributed in a way that promotes the survival of the collective.

History: There is no meaning in history. It is nothing more than a record of the natural operation of the natural universe.

Education: The primary function of education is to promote the survival of the collective.

What Have You Learned?
What have you learned here that will help you be more effective in your witness to the world?

Close the Session with prayer ... that God will give each of us
- the wisdom necessary to use today's material in ways that help each of us become more knowledgeable about our own faith,
- the understanding necessary to become more effective in their witness to those whom they know are not believers,
  —and—
- ... other prayer needs of the group or its members.

Session IV: *The Animistic Worldview*
A Study Session in one part on: *The Truth Mirage*, Chapter 7

Open the Session with prayer ... that God will give each of us
- the wisdom necessary to use today's material in ways that help each of us become more knowledgeable about our own faith,
  —and—
- the understanding necessary to become more effective in their witness to those whom they know are not believers.

Review ... ask the participants:
- What did you learn in last week's session that you did not know before?
- How might you—or have you already—applied your new knowledge in your life?
- What impact would this have—or, already did this have—on the way you lived out your faith in your daily life?

The Animistic Worldview (Chapter 7)

Opening the Conversation: ...
With our opening considerations of this Part/Chapter, how did the Apostle Paul (in Acts 17, see the passage as presented in the Session 2 and 3 material) frame his interactions for the animistic idol worshippers in the Athens Areopagus ... so they might understand his preaching? (He used one of their own gods as a point of contact to then tell them about the true God.)

Discussion Questions

1. *What is the most basic premise of Animism?*
   Animism is the belief that there exists a material world and a spirit world that symbiotically interact with one another. What happens in one part affects what happens in the other part.

2. *How do Animists deal with the three essential worldview questions?*
   a. The universe contains both material and immaterial parts. Spirits exist in a separate place from physical beings, but they interact with each other in a symbiotic relationship.
   b. Humans are material creatures who inhabit the physical world and have a spiritual core. At death, an individual's spirit enters the spiritual dimension.
   c. The most important thing for a person to strive for in this life is to take care of the obligations that keep the spirit beings satisfied.

3. *What would you expect Animists to think about Christianity and why?*
   You would expect Animists to believe Christianity is a false religion because it does not correspond with what they understand to be reality.

4. *Pick one of the following topics and explain how Animism would deal with it.*

   Theology: There are many gods/spirits in the spirit world that interact symbiotically with people in the material world.

   Philosophy:
     a. All of reality is symbiotically connected.
     b. Knowledge is not typically analyzed to understand why it exists, it is simply accepted as a human capability.
     c. Values are innate elements of reality that can be discovered by observing nature.

   Anthropology: Human beings are material creatures with a spiritual core. Human social organization revolves around the family and the clan.

   Sociology: Relationships need to be maintained across the entire material-spirit spectrum. This involves maintaining proper relationships within the family and clan, as well as with the spirits in the transcendent world.

   Psychology: Psychological problems are generally understood as some kind of action caused by the spirits in response to improper deeds done by humans.

   Communication: Communication involves interactions between human beings, and also with the spirits.

   Ethics and Morality: Acts that disrupt the smooth operation of the material and spirit worlds are considered immoral.

   Biology:
     a. Generally, the origin of life in animistic groups is expressed using mythological tales. Each group tends to have its own story.
     b. Animists don't typically consider the reason for the existence of various life forms. They simply recognize their existence.
     c. Animists typically have a high regard for life as they see all of life as symbiotically connected.

Law: Law is based on what a particular group understands will maintain harmony in the world.

Politics: Politics are generally exercised within the context of family, tribe, or clan. Leadership tends to emerge naturally as people age or through some royal line.

Economics: Animistic economies generally work on the basis of shared resources as people use the resources necessary for their survival.

History: History and tradition are the sources for an animistic understanding of reality. Knowledge of history is generally passed down via stories that are used to pass on an understanding of morality from generation to generation.

Education: Education in animistic societies is generally attained in the process of living life, with the older generations passing on essential knowledge to the younger generation.

What Have You Learned?
What have you learned here that will help you be more effective in your witness to the world?

Close the Session with prayer ... that God will give each of us
- the wisdom necessary to use today's material in ways that help each of us become more knowledgeable about our own faith,
- the understanding necessary to become more effective in their witness to those whom they know are not believers,
  —and—
- ... other prayer needs of the group or its members.

Session V: *The Far Eastern Thought Worldview*
A Study Session in one part on: *The Truth Mirage*, Chapter 8

Open the Session with prayer ... that God will give each of us
- the wisdom necessary to use today's material in ways that help each of us become more knowledgeable about our own faith,
  —and—
- the understanding necessary to become more effective in their witness to those whom they know are not believers.

Review ... ask the participants:
- What did you learn in last week's session that you did not know before?
- How might you—or have you already—applied your new knowledge in your life?
- What impact would this have—or, already did this have—on the way you lived out your faith in your daily life?

The Far Eastern Thought Worldview (Chapter 8)

Opening the Conversation: ...
With our opening considerations of this Part/Chapter, how did the Apostle Paul (in Acts 17, see the passage as presented in the Session 2 and 3 material) frame his interactions for the Stoics—influenced by Far Eastern Thought—in the Athens' Areopagus ... so they might understand his preaching? (While the Stoics were not Animists, they were very familiar with animistic concepts as it was the dominant worldview in that part of the world at that time. Thus, Paul's use of an animistic concept would have been grasped by the Stoics.)

Discussion Questions

1. *What is the most basic premise of the Far Eastern thought worldview?*
   Far Eastern Thought is based on the belief that the material universe represents an illusory expression of reality. This is based on the fact that it is greatly separated from ultimate reality. The Far Eastern Thought system asserts that the personal and material aspects of reality, that we seem to experience in this world, are actually not real. Rather, ultimate reality exists and operates in an entirely different way. Ultimate reality is seen to be an impersonal life force that exists beyond the material universe and has no material or personal element to it.

2. *How do Far Eastern Thought believers understand the three essential worldview questions?*
   a. In Far Eastern Thought, ultimate reality consists of a life force that is both impersonal and immaterial.
   b. Mankind is understood to be an expression of the impersonal life force that has been successively reincarnated and finally reached the human level.
   c. The ultimate goal of life is to escape the oppressive material world and merge with the main body of the impersonal life force.

3. What would you expect Far Eastern Thought believers to think about Christianity and why?
You would expect Far Eastern Thought believers to believe Christianity is a false religion because it does not correspond with what they understand to be reality.

4. Pick one of the following topics and explain how Far Eastern Thought would deal with it.

Theology: There exists a transcendent reality, but there is no personal God. Reality acts mechanically and impersonally.

Philosophy:
   a. Ultimate reality is impersonal and immaterial. The natural universe is illusory because it appears to be personal and material.
   b. The origin of knowledge has no material basis. Any knowledge we seem to gain about ultimate reality is acquired based on personal experience.
   c. Values are founded upon karma and have no meaning in an ultimate sense, as ultimate reality is impersonal.

Anthropology: Human beings are illusory expressions of the impersonal life force.

Sociology: The structure and operation of society at any given point in time is the result of the operation of karma.

Psychology: Based on the operation of karma, every person is at a place in life where they are supposed to be. Dealing with psychological issues is a matter of helping people accept their place in life.

Communication: Communication is useful as people live this life, but has no ultimate meaning as ultimate reality is impersonal.

Ethics and Morality: Good is considered that which allows a person to gain good karma, and bad is that which causes a person to gain bad karma.

Biology:
   a. Life is an illusory expression of the impersonal life force.
   b. The variety of life forms is accounted for based on karma and reincarnation.
   c. Life has no real value as it is an illusory expression of an impersonal life force.

Law: Law should promote actions that advance good karma and discourage actions that advance bad karma.

Session Five

Politics: The focus of politics is to create a social environment where good karma can advance the various manifestations of the life force.

Economics: The economic system that exists in the world is the result of the action of karma which has brought society to its current point.

History: Ultimate reality is impersonal, so history has no ultimate meaning.

Education: Education can help people in their current material life, but has no ultimate value as ultimate reality is impersonal.

What Have You Learned?
What have you learned here that will help you be more effective in your witness to the world?

Close the Session with prayer ... that God will give each of us
- the wisdom necessary to use today's material in ways that help each of us become more knowledgeable about our own faith,
- the understanding necessary to become more effective in their witness to those whom they know are not believers,
  —and—
- ... other prayer needs of the group or its members.

The Truth Mirage Leadership Notes

Session VI: *The Theistic Worldview and Hybrid Belief Systems*
A Study Session in two parts on: *The Truth Mirage*, Chapters 9 and 10

Open the Session with prayer ... that God will give each of us
- the wisdom necessary to use today's material in ways that help each of us become more knowledgeable about our own faith,
  —and—
- the understanding necessary to become more effective in their witness to those whom they know are not believers.

Review ... ask the participants:
- What did you learn in last week's session that you did not know before?
- How might you—or have you already—applied your new knowledge in your life?
- What impact would this have—or, already did this have—on the way you lived out your faith in your daily life?

Part 1. The Theistic Worldview (Chapter 9)

Opening the Conversation: ...
With our opening considerations of this Part/Chapter, how did the Apostle Paul (in Acts 17, see the passage as presented in the Session 2 and 3 material) frame his interactions for the Believing Jews and Greeks in the Thessalonica synagogue and the Believing Jews in the synagogue in Berea, ... so they might understand his preaching? (These Believing Jews and Believing Greeks were already familiar with the basic theistic teachings Paul was sharing, so all he had to add to the Jewish scripture and the Good News they had already heard from Jerusalem's Pentecost returnees was how Christ was the ultimate fulfillment of God's already revealed plan. Scripture's prophecy leads to Jesus—Paul preaches that—'reasoning from the scriptures'.)

Discussion Questions

1. *What is the most basic premise of a theistic worldview?*
   Theism is the belief that there is an objectively real, infinite, and transcendent God who is responsible for creating and sustaining the material universe.

2. *How do Theists answer the three essential worldview questions?*
   a. Concerning ultimate reality, all Theists believe that there is an actual, infinite, and transcendent God, who is the Creator and Sustainer of the physical universe. Theists believe there is a spiritual part of reality where God exists that is located outside the physical universe.
   b. In Theism, mankind is understood to be a special creation of God. Man's purpose is to discern the purpose of God and live it out in this life. Upon physical death, it is believed that individuals will enter the part of the spiritual world that is appropriate based on how life was lived on earth.

    c. Theism affirms that the purpose of life is to discern the will of God and live it out on earth. Doing so faithfully will allow a person to enter eternity with God.

3. What would you expect various Theists to believe about Christianity and why?
You would expect Theists to believe that their particular form of Theism represents the truth and other forms do not.

4. Pick one of the following topics and explain it using a theistic understanding of reality.

Theology: There exists a transcendent God who is the creator and sustainer of the material universe.

Philosophy:
    a. There are both natural and transcendent parts of reality. The natural part was created by God and operates based on natural laws that God put in place. The transcendent part where God exists is not subject to natural laws.
    b. God is the ultimate source of knowledge. He created mankind with a capacity to gain and use knowledge. Some knowledge of the transcendent world can be known, but must be revealed by God.
    c. Values are founded upon the nature and will of God.

Anthropology: Human beings are persons created by God for his own purposes.

Sociology: Human beings live in a world that was created in a particular way, and they organize society based on the nature of the natural order.

Psychology: Human beings are persons created by God who have the ability to act based on free will and self-determination. The human soul contains a spiritual element that is also capable of interacting with God. Psychological problems are rooted in issues of rebellion against God, and can only be overcome by solving those rebellion issues.

Communication: Human beings were created by God with the capacity for self-consciousness and free will. As such, the communication that takes place between persons is essentially a spiritual process.

Ethics and Morality: There is such a thing as an objective right and wrong, good and evil, and it is specifically defined by God and revealed to mankind. Human beings must discern what that is and live by it.

Biology:
   a. The origin of life is the result of God's creative activity.
   b. God is the creator of all life forms. Evolutionary development does exist, but only as it pertains to micro-evolution.
   c. Mankind is a special creation of God. Life is valuable because it is valuable to God.

Law: Theists look to God to understand how the law should be expressed in order to create an orderly society. There exists an objective foundation for law that should not be violated. In an ultimate sense, it is based on what God has revealed to be right and wrong.

Politics: The management of governmental systems draw their basic principles from God's revelation.

Economics: The form of economic order influenced by Theism depends on the type of theistic system one is dealing with. Legalistic belief systems tend to be led by dictatorial leadership, and tend toward a command economy. Systems that view human beings as God's stewards tend toward free enterprise, as they put individual humans in a position to manage the material resources of society.

History: History is understood to operate in a linear fashion that moves from past to present to future in a non-repetitive fashion.

Education: The goal of education is to lead people to a greater understanding of God's will and ways.

Part 2. Hybrid Worldview Beliefs (Chapter 10)

Opening the Conversation: ...
With our opening considerations of this Part/Chapter, we noted that every worldview system literally contradicts every other worldview system. Thus, when people try to combine beliefs from two or more worldviews, there will necessarily be internal contradictions. It is easy to notice this in certain modern Hybrid belief systems. However, this same problem often happens unintentionally, when people claim to believe in Christ—yet live life "as if" certain beliefs from other worldviews are true. Have the group discuss for a moment (without naming names) people they know who claim to be Christians yet believe in the Theory of Evolution (a Naturalistic belief), or who self-identify as a Christian yet think biblically-defined sexual immorality is not immoral (also a belief from Naturalism).

Discussion Questions

1. *What is the greatest problem hybrid belief systems face?*
   Every hybrid system has some kind of catastrophic internal contradiction.

2. *How do people manage to overcome the biggest problem facing hybrid belief systems?*
   Human beings have an uncanny ability to overlook and live with even massive contradictions.

3. *What worldview category do hybrid belief systems fall into?*
   Hybrid belief systems do not fall into any particular worldview category. Each one consists of its own unique combination of beliefs from two or more of the worldview categories.

4. *Of the hybrid systems mentioned in chapter 10, which do you think is the most prominent? Which is the most accepted?*
   Allow the participants to make their own choice and discuss why they think what they do.

What Have You Learned?
What have you learned here that will help you be more effective in your witness to the world?

Close the Session with prayer ... that God will give each of us
- the wisdom necessary to use today's material in ways that help each of us become more knowledgeable about our own faith,
- the understanding necessary to become more effective in their witness to those whom they know are not believers,
  —and—
- ... other prayer needs of the group or its members.

Notes

The Truth Mirage Leadership Notes

Session VII: *Worldview Sources*
A Study Session in two parts on: *The Truth Mirage*, Chapters 11 and 12

Open the Session with prayer ... that God will give each of us
- the wisdom necessary to use today's material in ways that help each of us become more knowledgeable about our own faith,
  — and —
- the understanding necessary to become more effective in their witness to those whom they know are not believers.

Review ... ask the participants:
- What did you learn in last week's session that you did not know before?
- How might you — or have you already — applied your new knowledge in your life?
- What impact would this have — or, already did this have — on the way you lived out your faith in your daily life?

Part 1. How do People Arrive at a Worldview? (Chapter 11)

Opening the Conversation: ...
With our opening considerations of this Part/Chapter, can you think of instances in the Bible — and even in today's settings — where people stood / stand against the truth and even persecute those who follow God because of their strong commitment to their own beliefs? Why do these people feel so strongly about their own beliefs?

The questions remain: How does it happen that every individual has a set of worldview beliefs? Additionally, where do those beliefs come from? Since there are so many different beliefs in existence, how is it possible that every person is so convinced that his or her own is the truth?

Discussion Questions

1. *What is the default worldview of every person on earth?*
   The default of each person is the worldview of the people who raised them.

2. *Why would a clash of worldviews cause some people to convert to a different belief?*
   For whatever reason, when new beliefs that are unfamiliar to an individual are made to sound credible enough, it can cause them to doubt their own worldview beliefs. This can happen when an individual is not convinced as to "why" their own worldview beliefs are true.

3. *What is necessary if a person is going to make a deliberate choice about what worldview belief to follow?*
   In order to make a conscious, deliberate choice, a person must know the available options.

Part 2: Worldview Authority Sources (Chapter 12)

Opening the Conversation: ...
With our opening considerations of this Part/Chapter, can you identify a few of the non-biblical belief systems you see today and identify their authority sources? As you do, try to identify what worldview the authority sources are connected to.

Discussion Questions

1. *What are the four possible worldview authority sources and what distinguishes each one?*
    a. Human Reason: Human reason is the only possible authority source for naturalistic belief systems, since they don't acknowledge the possibility of a transcendent authority source.
    b. Tradition: Tradition is the primary authority source for animistic belief systems that look to the beliefs of the ancestors for answers. These have generally been passed on as stories that express their understanding of reality.
    c. Human Experience: Human Experience is the primary authority source for Far Eastern Thought belief systems. These faith systems don't recognize the possibility of obtaining objective, rational, information about reality, as ultimate reality is understood to be impersonal, and the natural universe is understood to be illusory.
    d. Revelation: Revelation is the authority source for theistic belief systems. These believe that God exists and is able to pass information about reality to humanity.

2. *Why is it important to distinguish between big-picture and small-picture authority sources?*
   Big picture authority sources relate specifically to worldview systems. Small picture authority sources relate primarily to the specific elements of particular belief systems.

What Have You Learned?
What have you learned here that will help you be more effective in your witness to the world?

Close the Session with prayer ... that God will give each of us
- the wisdom necessary to use today's material in ways that help each of us become more knowledgeable about our own faith,
- the understanding necessary to become more effective in their witness to those whom they know are not believers,
  —and—
- ... other prayer needs of the group or its members.

Session VII

The Truth Mirage Leadership Notes

Session VIII: *Evaluating for Truth - Lesson 1*
A Study Session in three parts on: *The Truth Mirage*, Chapters 13, 14, and 15

Open the Session with prayer ... that God will give each of us
- the wisdom necessary to use today's material in ways that help each of us become more knowledgeable about our own faith,
  —and—
- the understanding necessary to become more effective in their witness to those whom they know are not believers.

Review ... ask the participants:
- What did you learn in last week's session that you did not know before?
- How might you—or have you already—applied your new knowledge in your life?
- What impact would this have—or, already did this have—on the way you lived out your faith in your daily life?

Part 1: Evaluating for the Truth of a Worldview (Chapter 13)

Opening the Conversation: ...
With our opening considerations of this Part/Chapter, we are forced to acknowledge that there is a way reality is actually structured, and it is not structured any other way. What this means in practical terms is that everyone who understands reality to be something other than what it actually is, lives in a fantasy world. Since there are billions of people who adhere to each of the worldview categories, and every worldview literally contradicts every other one, there are necessarily billions of people who do not live by the truth. Discuss the implications of this as it relates to eternity, and to the need to share a witness for Christ out in the world.

Discussion Questions

1. *Why is it important for human experience and an individual's beliefs to match up?*
   A match is a strong indication that a particular set of beliefs correspond with the way reality is actually structured.

2. *What happens when human experience and individual beliefs don't match up?*
   When human experience and individual beliefs don't match up, it is an indication that something is wrong with the belief.

Part 2: Evaluating the Truth of Naturalism (Chapter 14)

Opening the Conversation: ...
With our opening considerations of this Part/Chapter, we want to be aware that Naturalism is the worldview system that now dominates all of the major institutions of American society (entertainment industry, education, news media, business, government, and even many churches and families). Discuss the specific influences Naturalism has in these areas of life.

Discussion Questions

1. *In what ways does naturalistic belief match up with human experience?*
   Naturalism matches up with human experience as it relates to matters that deal only with empirical knowledge of the natural universe.

2. *In what ways does naturalistic belief not match up with human experience?*
   Naturalism does not match up with human experience in those places where empirical science is unable to demonstrate the truth of particular naturalistic beliefs.

3. *What does the fact that there are places where naturalistic belief does and does not match up with human experience tell you about the viability of Naturalism?*
   The fact that there are places where human experience and naturalistic belief don't match up is an indication that there are serious problems with Naturalism.

Part 3: Evaluating the Truth of Animism (Chapter 15)

Opening the Conversation: ...
With our opening considerations of this Part/Chapter we can see some of the influences Animism has in American society. In recent years, the entertainment industry, in particular, has promoted animistic beliefs through some of its blockbuster movies. Can you think of any of these (*Harry Potter, Avatar, Coco*)? What influence do you think these movies have, particularly on our young people?

Discussion Questions

   1. *In what ways does animistic belief match up with human experience?*
      Animistic beliefs match up with human experience in places where Animists do not assert supernatural causation, and where it is possible to empirically verify that experience.

   2. *In what ways does animistic belief not match up with human experience?*
      Animistic beliefs do not match up with human experience in places where Animism asserts a supernatural cause regarding matters where there is a known natural cause.

   3. *What does the fact that there are places where animistic belief does and does not match up with human experience tell you about the viability of Animism?*
      The fact that there are places where human experience and animistic belief don't match up is an indication that there are serious problems with Animism.

What Have You Learned?
What have you learned here that will help you be more effective in your witness to the world?

Close the Session with prayer ... that God will give each of us
- the wisdom necessary to use today's material in ways that help each of us become more knowledgeable about our own faith,
- the understanding necessary to become more effective in their witness to those whom they know are not believers,
  —and—
- ... other prayer needs of the group or its members.

The Truth Mirage Leadership Notes

Session IX: *Evaluating for Truth - Lesson 2*
A Study Session in two parts on: *The Truth Mirage*, Chapters 16 and 17

Open the Session with prayer ... that God will give each of us
- the wisdom necessary to use today's material in ways that help each of us become more knowledgeable about our own faith,
  —and—
- the understanding necessary to become more effective in their witness to those whom they know are not believers.

Review ... ask the participants:
- What did you learn in last week's session that you did not know before?
- How might you—or have you already—applied your new knowledge in your life?
- What impact would this have—or, already did this have—on the way you lived out your faith in your daily life?

Part 1: Evaluating the Truth of Far Eastern Thought (Chapter 16)

Opening the Conversation: ...
With our opening considerations of this Part/Chapter, we noted that there are no places where Far Eastern Thought matches up with the way human beings actually experience the real world. However, this worldview system still seems to have a great appeal to many people. Perhaps the biggest blockbuster movie series of all time, Star Wars, is based on this worldview system. We also see a huge interest in Yoga and Buddhist meditation, and there are many people who believe Karma is an actual power. What evidence of the influence of Far Eastern Thought have you seen as you have interacted with people in your daily life?

Discussion Questions

1. *In what ways does Far Eastern Thought belief match up with human experience?*
   Far Eastern Thought does not match up with human experience at any point. Everything in the natural universe is understood to be illusory.

2. *In what ways does Far Eastern Thought belief not match up with human experience?*
   Far Eastern Thought does not match up with human experience at any point. Everything in the natural universe is understood to be illusory.

3. *What does the fact that there are no places where Far Eastern Thought belief matches up with human experience tell you about the viability of Far Eastern Thought?*
   The fact that there are no places where human experience and Far Eastern Thought belief match up is an indication that it is impossible for it to be a representation of the actual structure of reality.

Part 2: Evaluating the Truth of Theism (Chapter 17)

Opening the Conversation: ...
With our opening considerations of this Part/Chapter, we noted that Theism matches up with the way human beings actually experience the real world at every point. That said, there are numerous theistic belief systems that have different views of ultimate reality, mankind, and the ultimate a person can get out of life. How is it possible for Theism to be true, yet many theistic belief systems to not be true? (Even untrue belief systems can be based on a worldview category that is true.)

Discussion Questions

1. In what ways does theistic belief match up with human experience?
Theistic belief matches up with human experience at every point.

2. In what ways does theistic belief not match up with human experience?
There is not a place where the beliefs of Theism do not match up with human experience.

3. What does the fact that theistic beliefs match up with human experience at every point tell you about the viability of Theism?
The fact that theistic beliefs match up with human experience at every point is a powerful indication that Theism is the worldview system that represents the truth about reality.

What Have You Learned?
What have you learned here that will help you be more effective in your witness to the world?

Close the Session with prayer ... that God will give each of us
- the wisdom necessary to use today's material in ways that help each of us become more knowledgeable about our own faith,
- the understanding necessary to become more effective in their witness to those whom they know are not believers,
  —and—
- ... other prayer needs of the group or its members.

Notes

The Truth Mirage Leadership Notes

Session 8: *Understanding the Christian Worldview*
A Study Session in two parts on: *The Truth Mirage*, Chapters 18 and 19

Open the Session with prayer ... that God will give each of us
- the wisdom necessary to use today's material in ways that help each of us become more knowledgeable about our own faith,
  —and—
- the understanding necessary to become more effective in their witness to those whom they know are not believers.

Review ... ask the participants:
- What did you learn in last week's session that you did not know before?
- How might you—or have you already—applied your new knowledge in your life?
- What impact would this have—or, already did this have—on the way you lived out your faith in your daily life?

Part 1: The Structure of Truth – Biblical Christianity (Chapter 18)

Opening the Conversation: ...
With our opening considerations of this Part/Chapter, we have asserted that the beliefs of biblical Christianity are true. When we wish to share our faith with a non-believer, this is the information we must communicate. Why do you think it is important to share both the answers to the three worldview questions and the worldview context of the Bible when communicating to people about the Christian faith? (Non-believers need both the worldview context and the specific knowledge of salvation in order to truly understand the Christian gospel message.)

Discussion Questions

1. *What does the Bible teach about God?*
   The Bible teaches that the only true God is the one who is revealed in the Bible. The specific characteristics of God are described on pages 202 – 211 in the text.

2. *What does the Bible teach about humanity?*
   The Bible teaches that human beings are persons made in the image of God and are fallen. (See pages 202 – 219)

3. *What does the Bible teach about salvation?*
   The Bible teaches that Christian salvation is expressed as a process and consists of Justification, Sanctification, and Glorification. Anything different from that is not Christian salvation. (See page 212)

4. *Based on a narrative description, what is the big-picture context of reality?*
   The context of a biblical worldview is expressed as:
   Creation—>The Fall—>Life after the Fall—>Redemption—>Eternity

Part 2: Why Christians Believe Different Things (Chapter 19)

Opening the Conversation: ...
With our opening considerations of this Part/Chapter, what are some of the beliefs held by other Christian groups that make you uncomfortable (*e.g.,* speaking in tongues, use of modern music, predestination, baptismal method, *etc.*)? What is it about these beliefs that make you feel that way? What can you do to ease the discomfort you feel? (Understand the Christian worldview essentials, study to determine why what you believe is correct, and learn more about beliefs of those you disagree with and why those seem to be wrong.)

Discussion Questions

1. *What are the essentials of the Christian faith?*
    The essentials of the Christian faith are defined specifically by the way the Bible answers the three essential worldview questions.

2. *What kinds of non-essentials still tend to divide Christians and how can this be avoided?*
    Non-essentials that tend to divide Christians fall into two categories: preference issues and non-essential doctrinal issues. Preference issues include such things as: organizational structure, music tastes, worship style, etc. Non-essential doctrines include those that are not necessary for salvation. These include such things as belief about: eschatology, baptism, the Lord's Supper, tongues, predestination, proper day for worship, the use of makeup for women, and the like.

3. *What evidence exists that some who call themselves Christians are not?*
    As the Christian faith involves a life change, those who live in ways that contradict the moral teachings of the Bible give strong evidence that perhaps their lives have not been changed.

What Have You Learned?
What have you learned here that will help you be more effective in your witness to the world?

Close the Session with prayer ... ... that God will give each of us
- the wisdom necessary to use today's material in ways that help each of us become more knowledgeable about our own faith,
- the understanding necessary to become more effective in their witness to those whom they know are not believers,
    —and—
- ... other prayer needs of the group or its members.

Notes

# The Truth Mirage Leadership Notes

Session XI: *Using Worldview Knowledge in the World*
A Study Session in three parts on: *The Truth Mirage*, Chapters 20, 21, and 22

Open the Session with prayer … that God will give each of us
- the wisdom necessary to use today's material in ways that help each of us become more knowledgeable about our own faith,
  — and —
- the understanding necessary to become more effective in their witness to those whom they know are not believers.

Review … ask the participants:
- What did you learn in last week's session that you did not know before?
- How might you — or have you already — applied your new knowledge in your life?
- What impact would this have — or, already did this have — on the way you lived out your faith in your daily life?

Part 1: What Does Worldview Conflict Look Like? (Chapter 20)

Opening the Conversation: …
With our opening considerations of this Part/Chapter,
- Name some of the kinds of conflicts that are of little consequence, and discuss why they are not so important (*e.g.,* music preferences, sports preferences, technology preferences, *etc.*)
- Name some of the modern religious battles regarding beliefs that people are often willing to even go to war over and discuss why they are important. (*e.g.,* Moral beliefs, political beliefs, education philosophy, *etc.*)

Discussion Questions

1. *What is the difference between culture wars and worldview wars?*
   Culture war issues relate to conflicts that occur based on tensions due to outward cultural expressions. Worldview wars focus on the conflicting worldview beliefs that underlie the cultural conflicts.

2. *To really understand the issues that are fought over in the culture wars, what is necessary?*
   To understand the issues that are fought over in the culture wars, a person needs to understand the underlying worldview beliefs at the root of the culture wars.

3. *How can culture wars actually be won?*
   Winning culture wars requires a change of heart and mind.

The Truth Mirage Leadership Notes

Part 2: How Can Christians Be Sure They Hold a Biblical Worldview? (Chapter 21)

Opening the Conversation: ...
With our opening considerations of this Part/Chapter, does it make you more confident in your own Christian faith knowing that "those who answer the three worldview questions based on biblical teachings are the ones who hold a biblical worldview?" Why or why not? (Because the three worldview questions are so important in understanding worldview concepts, have the members quote them and discuss among themselves their meaning.)

Discussion Questions

   1. *How does the Bible answer the three essential worldview questions?*
      a. What Is the Nature of Ultimate Reality? A biblical worldview points to the God of the Bible as the foundation for ultimate reality. In particular, the Bible teaches that God exists as a Trinitarian being who is holy, just, and love—all three at the same time.
      b. What is a Human Being? The Bible teaches that man is a special creation of God who was created in His image, but is fallen.
      c. What Is the Ultimate a Human Being Can Get Out of this Life? (Salvation) God's original purpose for the creation of mankind was for Him to be able to enjoy an intimate personal relationship with humanity. Salvation is, then, the restoration of that relationship. It is accomplished when individuals open their lives to Christ by placing their faith in Him for their salvation.

   2. *What does a person's lifestyle tell you about their worldview beliefs?*
      Every person outwardly expresses their worldview beliefs. Those who truly believe the God of the Bible exists, and who have come to actually know him in a personal relationship, will live life based on that understanding of reality. (See Matthew 7:16-20 and have it ready.)

   3. *How does God work in individual believer's lives to equip them to carry out His will in daily life?*
      God, by his Spirit, lives in every believer's life and provides power to live out His will.

Part 3: How Can Christians Effectively Fight the Worldview War? (Chapter 22)

Opening the Conversation: ...
With our opening considerations of this Part/Chapter in mind, we see that worldview conflicts are battles over the heart, mind, and soul of human beings. Look at Acts 17:16-34. What tools did Paul employ to fight his own worldview war? (He used his knowledge of their beliefs to craft a message that they could understand, and used that as a tool to explain the God of the Bible.)

Have the participants bring up the situations and subjects which involve worldview conflict that still make them uncomfortable (*e.g.,* Loudmouth militant Atheists, Abortion, Homosexual marriage, *etc.*). Have the group figure out together what would be necessary to resolve this discomfort.

Discussion Questions

1. *What is the essential knowledge base Christians must possess to fulfill God's purpose in life?*
   To fulfill God's purpose in life, a person must know God's revelation.

2. *What kinds of skills are necessary for Christians to develop in order to fulfill God's purpose in life?*
   In order to fulfill God's purpose for our lives, Christians must know how to share their faith, as well as become proficient in the skills related to one's spiritual gifts.

3. *How does one go about developing an individual plan for accomplishing the will of God in life?*
   For an individual to develop a plan for accomplishing God's will, one must become intentional in understanding God's purpose, and work to fulfill it.

4. *What must a person ultimately be willing to do in order to accomplish God's purpose?*
   In order to accomplish God's purpose, an individual must ultimately be willing to put himself under the lordship of Christ and actually engage the work of ministry.

What Have You Learned?
What have you learned here that will help you be more effective in your witness to the world?

Preparation for Next Week
Tell each person in the group to search news sites and bring two articles with them next week that have to do with worldview issues. These articles can be about how various moral issues are expressed in society, explanations of various religions, cults or philosophies that are being promoted in society, or beliefs being promoted in politics, the media, education, business, entertainment, family, or religion. Explain that the group will be discussing these articles during class next week.

Close the Session with prayer … that God will give each of us
- the wisdom necessary to use today's material in ways that help each of us become more knowledgeable about our own faith,
- the understanding necessary to become more effective in their witness to those whom they know are not believers,
  —and—
- … other prayer needs of the group or its members.

Notes

The Truth Mirage Leadership Notes

Session XII: *Putting it All Together*
A Study Session in one part on: *The Truth Mirage*

Open the Session with prayer ... that God will give each of us
- the wisdom necessary to use today's material in ways that help each of us become more knowledgeable about our own faith,
  —and—
- the understanding necessary to become more effective in their witness to those whom they know are not believers.

Review ... ask the participants:
- What did you learn in last week's session that you did not know before?
- How might you — or have you already — applied your new knowledge in your life?
- What impact would this have — or, already did this have — on the way you lived out your faith in your daily life?

Opening the Conversation: ...
With our opening considerations of this whole book, *The Truth Mirage*, in mind, take a few moments to allow the class members to dialog about the various elements of worldview that have been studied in this book (see their consideration list on this Study Session's page). Have the class discuss how all the parts go together.

With the four worldview category differences in mind, let's watch and learn the master evangelist in action once again. (Read, or have a group member read, the Acts 17 passage in the Participant's Session 12 material — out loud for the group / the more impassioned, the better).

And in Acts 17:16-20, see also the explanatory material opposite the passage in Session 2

Have the group review how the Apostle Paul framed his interactions differently for:
- the Believing Jews and Greeks in the Thessalonica synagogue,
- the Believing Jews in the synagogue in Berea, and
- the various believers in Athens
    - animistic idol worshippers,
    - the naturalistic Epicurean philosophers,
    - the pantheistic Stoics

... that they might understand his preaching.

How might we use Paul's approaches today as we encounter this diversity of worldview categories and the belief systems that rest on them?

Discussion

The "content-in-real-life" discussion this week will be about the articles people bring to class with them. Be prepared with a hand-full of articles yourself in case some forget to bring them. Have the individuals summarize their article and share what they got out of them based on their worldview training. From the articles, discuss: authority source, worldview beliefs, evaluation of truth, and how Christians can interact with this topic in order to express their Christian faith.

What Have You Learned?
What have you learned here that will help you be more effective in your witness to the world?

Close the Session with prayer ... that God will give each of us
- the wisdom necessary to use today's material in ways that help each of us become more knowledgeable about our own faith,
- the understanding necessary to become more effective in their witness to those whom they know are not believers,
  —and—
- ... other prayer needs of the group or its members.

Notes

The Truth Mirage Leadership Notes

CONGRATULATIONS!

And a big *thank-you* for completing your group leadership study of
The Truth Mirage.

Without your hard work through this study, all of our hard work in producing it goes for naught.

We try to make your personal preparations and group study experience as profitable for you as we can—but we know that your experience with it, with your group, and its materials can add even more benefit to others who will follow you in this and other studies we produce.

Would you share with us what we could do to improve our courseware?

Please share your suggestions with the Authors and Editors at **LeadershipBooks.Net** that we may fold them into this and following works to make your and your fellow participants and leaders experience with our materials more fulfilling.

Just visit our contact page, **LeadershipBooks.Net** (click on: CONTACT US) and share with us right on this page, send us a letter—or email us with your suggestions!

All comments are welcome and will help us produce better books, study guides, and video supplements.

Thank you for your feedback comments—and for working your way through *The Truth Mirage* and its study. Our prayers are with you that you may use its content in your own life to understand the many ways the world understands reality and how this affects our ability to understand each other—as those worldviews that used to be way out in the foreign mission field are now all right here among us!

www.ingramcontent.com/pod-product-compliance
Lightning Source LLC
Chambersburg PA
CBHW080717130526
44591CB00046BA/2480